SUPERSCIENCE

SOLIDS, LIQUIDS AND GASES

Rob Colson

W

FRANKLIN WATTS

This edition published in 2013 by
Franklin Watts
338 Euston Road
London NW1 3BH

Franklin Watts Australia
Level 17/207 Kent Street
Sydney NSW 2000

Produced for Franklin Watts by
Tall Tree Ltd

Editor: Jon Richards
Designer: Jonathan Vipond
Photographer: Ed Simkins
Consultant: Ade Deane-Pratt

A CIP catalogue record for this book is available
from the British Library.

Dewey Classification 530.4

ISBN 978 1 4451 2294 6

Printed in China

Franklin Watts is a division of Hachette Children's
Books, an Hachette UK company.

www.hachette.co.uk

Picture credits:
Cover: main Vladimir Seliverstov/Dreamstime.
com, tl Natalya Aleksahina/Dreamstime.com tm A
Cerar/Dreamstime.com, tr Can Balcioglu/
Dreamstime.com 1 Michael Sheehan/Dreamstime.
com, 3 Raymond Kasprzak/Dreamstime.com, 4r
Stepan Popov/Dreamstime.com, 4m Michael
Dykstra | Dreamstime.com, 4l Ggw1962/
Dreamstime.com, 5 Olga Milkina/istockphoto, 6
istockphoto, 7t Nataliya Evmenenko/Dreamstime.
com, 7b istockphoto, 8 Suprijono Suharjoto/
Dreamstime.com, 9t Viktorfischer/Dreamstime.
com, 9b Davinci/Dreamstime.com, 10 Alistair
Scott/Dreamstime.com, 11t kieran mithani/
istockphoto, 11b USAF, 12 Michael Sheehan/
Dreamstime.com, 13 Pudiyapura/Dreamstime.
com, 14 NASA, 15 Pete Favelle/Dreamstime.com,
16 Shvetic/Dreamstime.com. 17t Valeria
Cantone/Dreamstime.com, 18 Melissa King/
Dreamstime.com, 19t Shawn Henning/ GNU
Sharealike, 19b Hustvedt/ GNU Sharealike, 20
Michelle Bergkamp/Dreamstime.com, 21
Dreamstime.com, 22 Alfonso D'agostino/
Dreamstime.com, 23t RTimages/ istockphoto.com,
23b Raymond Kasprzak/Dreamstime.com, 24
Adeline Yeo Hwee Ching/Dreamstime.com, 25t
Simone van Den Berg/Dreamstime.com, 26
Lanalanglois/Dreamstime.com, 27t Renzzo/
Dreamstime.com, 27b Noodle snacks/GNU, 28
Kevin Panizza/Dreamstime.com, 29t Matthias
Kabel/GNU Sharealike, 29b Kinlem/Dreamstime.
com

✳ Contents

*States of matter

The stuff from which everything is made is called matter. Matter exists in three different forms, called states: solids, liquids and gases. Each state has very different qualities.

▮ The three states

Solids keep their size and shape. Some solids, such as stone, are very hard. Other solids, such as a lump of cheese, may be very soft. Liquids, such as water or oil, keep the same volume, but take on the shape of the container they are in. Gases, such as the air, spread out all around us. Liquids and gases are called fluids because they flow.

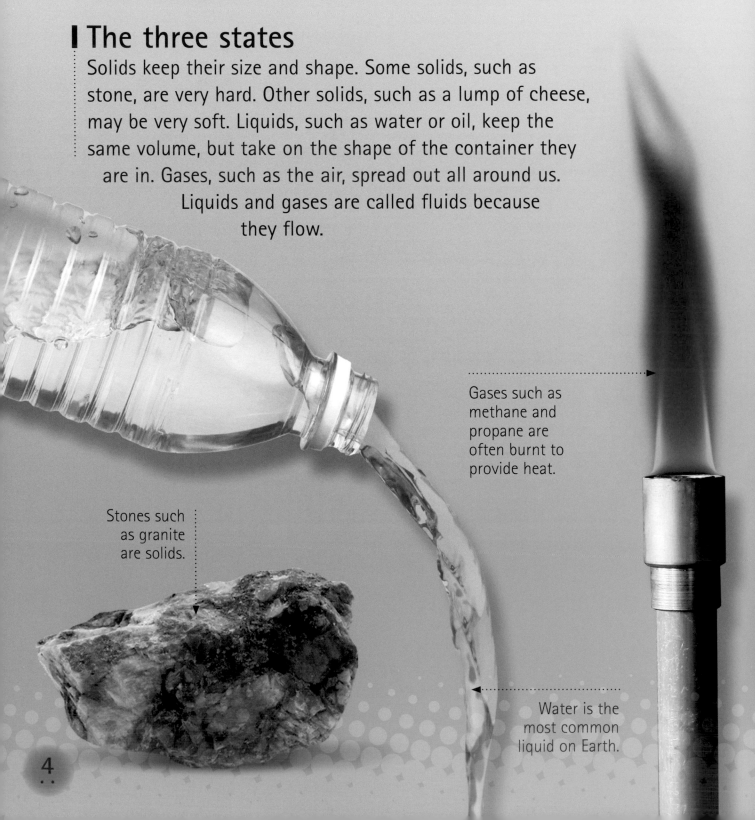

Gases such as methane and propane are often burnt to provide heat.

Stones such as granite are solids.

Water is the most common liquid on Earth.

Changing states

Matter changes from one state to another as it is heated or cooled. The hotter a substance is, the more energy it contains. At its coolest, all matter is solid. When it is heated, it gains energy, and turns first into a liquid and then into a gas. Gases have the most energy of all, so be careful around boiling water. As the water is heated, it turns into the hot gas steam, which has enough energy to rise up into your face and scald you.

The steam rising from boiling water mixes with the cooler air above, causing a fine mist made of tiny droplets of water.

Moving molecules

Matter is made from tiny particles called molecules, which themselves are made from smaller atoms. Molecules are much too small to see – you could fit up to a billion of them into the full-stop at the end of this sentence. In solids, the molecules are tightly packed together. In liquids, the extra energy in the molecules has weakened the bonds between them, and they move more freely. The molecules in gases are much farther away from each other and move around in all directions.

Solid

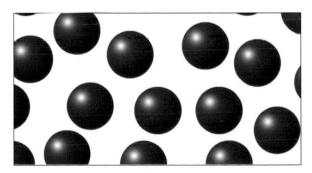

Liquid

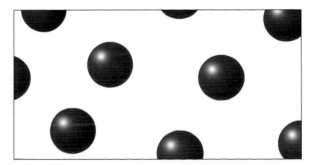

Gas

*What is a solid?

The molecules in a solid have strong bonds between them that hold them in place. The stronger the bond between the molecules, the harder the solid.

Crystals and glassy solids

The hardest solids are crystals. The hardest crystals of all, diamonds, are formed by huge pressures and high temperatures deep underground. The molecules in crystals are arranged in regular patterns, and their bonds can be very hard to break. The shape the crystals take reflects the way the atoms in the molecules are joined together. Solids with molecules that are not arranged in a regular pattern are known as glassy solids.

Diamonds are the hardest crystals of all. They are so hard that they are used on the tips of the drills working on oil rigs, such as this one.

Modelling clay is a plastic solid, which can be made into lots of different shapes.

Changing shape

Solids change shape or break when a force squashes or stretches them. Sometimes solids keep their new shape when the force is removed. This is called being plastic. Modelling clay is a plastic solid that can easily be squeezed or stretched into new shapes. Other solids go back to their original shape when the force is removed. This is called being elastic. A tennis ball is elastic. Squash a tennis ball in your hand. It will become a sphere again as soon as you stop squashing it.

Brittle solids

Instead of changing shape, some solids break when force is applied to them. These solids are called brittle, and they usually make a 'snap' sound when they break. A bar of chocolate is brittle, and you can easily break a piece off to eat. Other solids break only when a large force is applied to them. Glass is much more difficult to break than chocolate, but when it does break, it often shatters into many pieces. Solids that shatter like this can be very dangerous as the broken pieces often have hard, sharp edges.

This glass has broken into several pieces. Each of the pieces of broken glass has sharp edges that could easily cause a nasty cut.

*What is a liquid?

The bonds between the molecules in a liquid are weaker than those in a solid. A liquid spreads out to take the shape of the container it is in.

▮ A fixed volume

A liquid takes the shape of its container, but may not fill it: the liquid forms a horizontal surface within the container. This happens because a liquid keeps a fixed volume, and the force of gravity makes it fill a container from the bottom up. Unlike solids and gases, liquids are wet, which means that some of their molecules may stick to solid surfaces. This is why your skin is covered in water when you climb out of a swimming pool.

The water in a glass takes on the shape of the glass but has a horizontal surface. The surface stays horizontal when you tilt the glass. This is due to the force of gravity pulling the water down.

Project Dissolving

Fill a cup or glass nearly to the brim with warm water. Carefully pour a teaspoon of sugar into the water and stir it gently so that the sugar dissolves. Keep adding sugar one spoonful at a time. The sugar molecules separate to fill gaps between the water molecules and form a solution. The first two or three spoonfuls will not make the water level rise. Only once those gaps have been filled will the water rise and spill over the top of the cup. Now add a spoonful of sand to a glass of water. The grains of sand do not dissolve, but are held in the water in suspension. The molecules in the grains stay together, and the water level rises immediately.

The first couple of spoonfuls of sugar dissolve without making the water level rise at all.

Thick and thin

Liquids flow from one place to another under the influence of gravity. Some liquids flow more quickly than others. Thin liquids such as water flow easily. Thick liquids such as honey or treacle flow much more slowly. The more slowly a liquid flows, the more 'viscous' it is said to be. In an experiment at the University of Queensland in Australia, a highly viscous liquid called pitch has been flowing out of a tube at a rate of one drop per decade since 1927. The pitch is 230 billion times more viscous than water!

Lava is the molten rock that flows out of a volcano. It is very viscous and flows down a hillside much more slowly than a stream of water.

*What is a gas?

The molecules in a gas are spaced out a long way from each other. A gas does not stay in one place or keep the same volume, but spreads out across space. We are surrounded by a gas all the time – air.

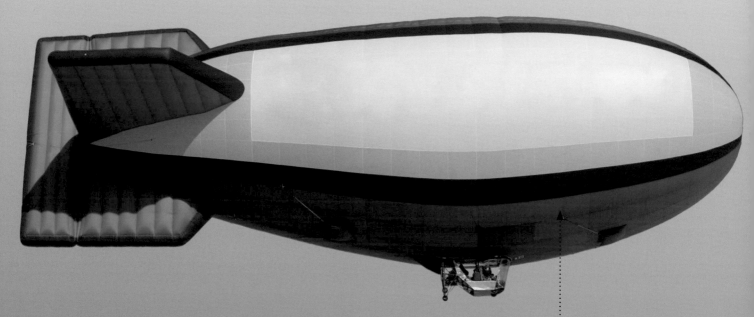

Building pressure

The molecules in a gas have a great deal of energy and zoom around in all directions at high speed. Since the molecules are a long way from each other, you often cannot see or feel a gas, although you can sometimes smell it. A gas contained within an enclosed container causes outward pressure. The pressure is caused by gas molecules bumping into the container. If the container is made of an elastic solid, the pressure from the gas will cause it to inflate. This is what happens when you blow up a balloon.

An airship is filled with the gas helium. The pressure from the gas gives the airship its shape. Helium is lighter than air, so the airship floats.

Diffusion

Gases in the same space mix with each other in a process called diffusion. Liquids can also mix by diffusion. When you spray a little perfume into the air, the gas from the perfume will at first be concentrated in a small area around you. It will then spread out and mix with the air until the concentration of the perfume is the same throughout the room. Diffusion is caused by the random movement of molecules. This random movement can also cause gases to move through tiny gaps in solid surfaces. A balloon will eventually deflate as the air inside it passes through the rubber.

A balloon slowly deflates as the air inside it passes through the rubber.

Plasma

The Northern Lights can be seen at night near the North Pole. The spectacular light display occurs when plasma from the Sun collides with atoms and molecules in the Earth's upper atmosphere.

Plasma is a special state of gas sometimes called the fourth state of matter. Gas becomes plasma when it takes on an electrical charge. An atom contains positively charged protons and negatively charged electrons. The atoms in a gas contain the same number of protons and electrons, so have no overall charge. In plasma, some of the electrons become detached from their atoms. The atoms are now known as ions. The ions contain more protons than electrons and are positively charged. The electrons are free to move, which means that the plasma can conduct electricity. Stars are made from plasma, and it is the most common state of matter in the universe.

*Fluids and waves

A fluid is any state of matter that can flow from one place to another. Gases and liquids are fluids. Solids are not fluids but sometimes behave as if they were.

Making waves

Energy is transferred through fluids in waves. Ocean waves are caused by the force of the wind blowing over the surface of the water. The energy from the wind is transferred to the water. The water carries the energy along in the wave. The water moves up and down where it is, but the waves may be carried for thousands of miles. The farther a wave has travelled, the larger it can become, and surfers choose beaches facing a wide ocean to find the biggest waves to ride. Once the wave reaches shallow water, it breaks and the water comes crashing down. Surfers ride the waves as they break.

Surfers ride waves as they break when they approach the beach. Surfers keep a close eye on the weather forecast to see which beaches will have the biggest waves.

Sand dunes

Solids may form themselves into waves when they are made from millions or billions of tiny pieces. The wind causes sand to form waves called dunes. The grains of sand on the side of the dune that faces the wind are moved up to the top by a process called saltation. The wind lifts the grains into the air then drops them a little farther up the slope. When they hit the ground, they bump into other grains, which jump up and are themselves caught by the wind. When the sand grains fall over the crest of the dune, they pile up. Eventually gravity causes the sand in the pile to slip down to the bottom in small avalanches. In this way, the dunes slowly move in the direction of the wind.

The large sand dunes of the Sahara Desert move a few metres each year.

Project **Testing viscosity**

Some liquids flow more easily than others. To test this, fill a series of four jars with different liquids. You could try water, cooking oil, milk and washing-up liquid. With a partner, hold four identical marbles, one in each hand, and drop them from the same height into each jar. Watch the marbles sink to the bottom and rank each liquid in order according to how long it took the marble to reach the bottom. The longer it took, the more viscous the liquid, which means that it flowed out of the way of the marble more slowly. If you look at the surface of each jar, you will see ripples, tiny waves made by the marbles when they hit the surface.

*Freezing

When a liquid is cooled, it changes state from a liquid to a solid. The temperature at which this happens is known as the freezing point.

Uranus

Neptune

The planets Uranus and Neptune are known as the 'Ice Giants'. They are very cold planets and their atmospheres contain frozen water, methane and ammonia.

Freezing point

Once a liquid has been cooled to its freezing point, it will stay at that temperature until all the liquid has turned into a solid. Only once it is totally solid can it get any colder. Heat must continue to be removed from the liquid or it will stop freezing, so a freezing liquid actually gives off heat! Sometimes a liquid can be cooled to below its freezing point without freezing. This is called supercooling. When supercooled water droplets in clouds finally freeze, they form ice crystals, which stick to each other to make snowflakes.

Freezing water

When a liquid freezes into a solid, it becomes smaller and more dense. The only exception to this is water, which expands and becomes less dense when it turns into ice. This is why icebergs float and also why pipes can crack when the water in them freezes during winter. The covering of floating ice on the frozen Arctic Ocean is between 2 and 5 metres thick. This layer of ice protects the liquid below from the cold air, which is just as well for the fish and other creatures that live in the water.

Project Making ice

Half-fill a plastic bottle with water, and mark on the side of the bottle the level of the water. Stand the bottle upright in the freezer and leave it to freeze for a few hours. When you come back, check the level of the ice against the mark. Ice is approximately 9 per cent less dense than water, so the level will have risen by about a tenth. This means that, if you fill a container more than 90 per cent with water and freeze it, the container will break, so you have to be very careful what you put in the freezer.

Huge icebergs float on water because ice is less dense than water.

*Melting

When a solid is heated, it changes into a liquid. The temperature at which this happens is known as the melting point, and is usually the same as the freezing point. Melting is the reverse of freezing.

Casting shapes

Hard solids such as metals are made into all kinds of shapes in a process called casting. The metal is heated until it melts. The liquid metal is then poured into a mould with a hollow space in it that is the desired shape. As the metal is liquid, it takes the shape of the hollow space. The metal is left to cool and turns back into a solid. The mould is then broken to reveal the metal casting inside. Other solids such as concrete, plaster and plastic are also made into different shapes by casting.

Molten steel is made in a steelworks. The melting point of steel is about 1400°C. The melted metal is then cast into different shapes.

Skaters wear skates with narrow edges, which melt the ice as the skater moves.

Under pressure

Energy is needed to break the bonds of a solid and turn it into a liquid. This energy can be provided by heat, and it can also be provided by pressure. The energy from the pressure transfers to the solid's molecules and heats them up. Put a solid under enough pressure, and it will melt. Skaters use pressure to move across the ice. The pressure from the weight of the skater is concentrated in the narrow edge of the skate. This melts the ice under the skate, providing a film of water for the skater to glide over. That is as close to walking on water as we can get!

Project Solids and liquids

Apart from ice, all solids expand when they melt. To see this in action, melt some butter in a pan, stirring it until it has totally melted. Be sure not to heat it too quickly or it will burn. Pour the butter into a small, narrow jar. Fill the jar right to the top and put it in the refrigerator for a couple of hours to cool and solidify. When you take the jar out, you will see that there is now a small hole in the middle of the butter. This is because the solid butter now takes up less space than the melted butter that you poured into the jar.

A hole forms in the middle of the butter as it starts to solidify on the outside first.

Evaporation and boiling

Liquids turn into a gas when they are heated to their boiling point. Cool liquids can also turn to gas by the process of evaporation.

Sheets on a line dry by evaporation. They dry more quickly when there is a breeze to carry the water vapour away.

Evaporation

If you leave a saucer of water in the sun, the water disappears in a few hours. It has changed into the gas water vapour and mixed with the air in a process known as evaporation. The molecules in a liquid do not all have the same energy, and the more energetic molecules can escape into the air from the water surface. The warmer the liquid becomes, the more energy the molecules have and the faster it will evaporate. The evaporation of water also depends on how much water vapour is already in the air, known as humidity. At 100 per cent humidity, air cannot hold more water vapour and evaporation stops.

Sublimation

As dry ice sublimates, the very cold carbon dioxide gas cools the air, causing water vapour to condense into clouds (see page 20 for more on condensation).

Some substances turn straight from a solid to a gas without passing through a liquid state. This is called sublimation. When a gas turns directly into a solid, the process is called deposition. Solid carbon dioxide sublimates at room temperature. It is known as dry ice because it is dry to touch. But do not touch it as it is very very cold at -78°C, and at this temperature, a substance actually feels like it is burning. Dry ice is used to keep food cold without getting it wet. It is also used on stage to provide the effect of smoke without choking the actors.

Boiling point

When a liquid is heated to its boiling point, it turns to a gas very quickly. Further heating does not increase the temperature of the liquid, but merely speeds up the rate at which it turns to a gas. At normal air pressure, the boiling point of water is 100°C. If you decrease the pressure of the air around the water, the boiling point also decreases. At high altitudes, the air is thinner and air pressure is lower, so water boils at a lower temperature. A pressure cooker increases the air pressure by sealing air and water into the pan, so water reaches up to 120°C.

Water can reach 120°C in a pressure cooker, so food cooks more quickly.

*Condensation

Condensation is the reverse of evaporation, as a substance changes from a gas to a liquid state. The liquid produced is called the condensate.

▌The dew point

The temperature at which water vapour in the air condenses into a liquid is called the dew point. This temperature varies according to the humidity and pressure of the air. The higher the pressure, the higher the dew point. Increasing humidity also raises the dew point. A gas needs a surface onto which it will condense. Water vapour in the air condenses onto plants and other surfaces as dew when the temperature drops at night. Vapour also condenses around tiny particles suspended in the air, such as pollen and dust, to make the droplets of water that form clouds.

Dew forms on plants when the temperature falls at night.

Distillation

The processes of evaporation and condensation are used in many different industries as part of a process called distillation. Mixed liquids can be separated from each other by distillation if the liquids have different boiling points. The mixture is heated to the boiling point of one of the liquids, called the distillate, which boils off and is then cooled and condensed back into another container. This process is used to separate crude oil and to produce strong alcoholic drinks such as whisky.

Clouds form from water vapour that has condensed into droplets. High clouds are made of tiny ice crystals, which form in the very low temperatures at high altitudes.

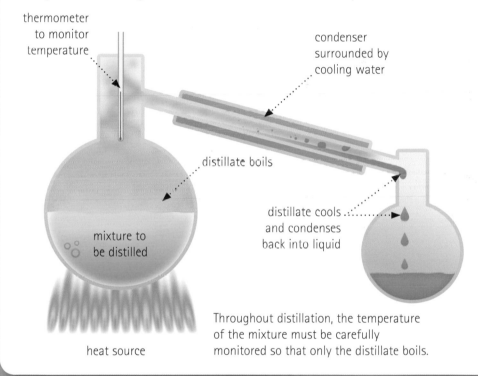

thermometer to monitor temperature

condenser surrounded by cooling water

distillate boils

mixture to be distilled

distillate cools and condenses back into liquid

heat source

Throughout distillation, the temperature of the mixture must be carefully monitored so that only the distillate boils.

The water cycle

Water vapour condenses into droplets in the air to form clouds. When the droplets grow large enough, they fall from the sky as rain or snow. The rainwater drains into rivers and the oceans or is taken up by plants, and evaporates back into the air as vapour. The water vapour then condenses once more into clouds. This continuous process is known as the water cycle, and is crucial to all life on Earth. The water cycle is driven by the energy of the Sun, which warms the oceans to cause the evaporation that starts the process.

Solutions and mixtures

Substances that are mixed together to form a consistent new mixture are called solutions. Liquids can form solutions with other liquids, solids and gases.

▌Mineral deposits

Water in nature is never pure. It is a solution with many different minerals in it. When you boil water, it leaves behind deposits of these minerals, called limescale. The build-up of limescale can be seen inside kettles, which have to be cleaned every so often to keep them working efficiently. The evaporation of dripping water inside caves over thousands of years can leave behind spectacular deposits of minerals in the form of long, thin spikes. Spikes that hang from the roof of the cave where the drops form are called stalactites. Spikes that stick up from the ground where the drops fall are called stalagmites.

These cave stalactites have formed from calcium carbonate deposits.

Paints

Paints are mixtures of different liquids. The paints that we use to decorate walls are mixtures called emulsions. The liquids in an emulsion do not mix evenly. Instead, tiny droplets of one liquid are held in suspension, or floating, in another liquid. The colour pigment in emulsion paint is suspended in water. After the paint has been applied to a wall, the water evaporates as it dries, leaving behind the pigment, which hardens to a solid and sticks to the wall surface.

Emulsion paints are not solutions: they are mixtures of liquid pigment and water.

Fizzy drinks

Fizzy drinks are made by dissolving the gas carbon dioxide in water to form a solution. The gas is dissolved into the water by combining them under pressure. As long as the drink stays in an airtight container, the gas stays dissolved, but as soon as you open the can or bottle, the pressure is released and the gas escapes from the water as bubbles, which are less dense than the liquid and rise quickly through it. Once all the carbon dioxide has left the water, the drink goes flat.

When lots of gas rises to the top, the drink forms a froth of bubbles.

*Water

Water is a very special substance, the only one that occurs naturally on Earth in all three states of matter. It is vital to life and readily dissolves other substances.

❙ Geysers

Water is found as a gas in the air, as a liquid in streams, rivers and the oceans, and as a solid high in the sky and around the North and South Poles. Liquid water at the Earth's surface can work its way down through the soil and rocks to a depth of up to 2,000 metres. In volcanic areas, the water may meet with the hot molten rocks of the Earth's interior deep under the surface. The water boils under the heat and pressure, and when the pressure reaches a critical level, the water erupts through the surface in a spectacular spray of steam and hot water, called a geyser. There are about 1,000 geysers in the world, and all of them erupt at regular intervals.

Geysers form when water seeps through soil and rock and is heated by molten rock deep inside the Earth.

It is important to drink plenty of water when we are losing it from our bodies as sweat.

Keeping our cool

Our bodies may seem solid, but they are mostly made of liquid water with other substances dissolved in it. We keep ourselves cool in hot weather by losing some of that water. Water passes through the skin at sweat glands. The water evaporates into the air from the surface of the skin. As the water molecules with the most energy escape into the air, they carry away heat, cooling us down. When we exercise in hot weather, we may lose several litres of water an hour by sweating, so it is very important that we replace the water by taking regular drinks.

Project Make an egg float

Eggs normally sink in water, but you can make them float by adding salt to the water. Half-fill a glass with warm water and drop an egg in it. The egg sinks to the bottom as it is more dense than the water. Now start adding salt to the water one tablespoon at a time. Stir well to help the salt dissolve. By dissolving salt in the water, you are making it more dense, and eventually the egg will float to the surface. Seawater has salt dissolved in it, which is why you float more easily in the sea. Some seas, such as the Dead Sea in Israel, are so salty that you do not sink at all.

Adding salt to water makes it more dense than an egg. An egg will float in salty water.

*Surface tension

Liquids form a boundary with the air at their surface. Forces at the surface, called surface tension, are responsible for the shape of raindrops, can make a glass of water bulge at the top, and also provide a home for small animals.

Held by a force

Molecules in a liquid are all attracted to each other by a force. The molecules underneath the surface are pulled in all directions by the molecules that surround them. But the molecules at the surface are only pulled by the molecules next to or underneath them. This inward force causes the liquid to form the shape that has the smallest surface area possible: a sphere. If you look at a newly polished car bonnet after some rain, the water forms tiny spherical beads on the waxy surface. The water cannot stick to the polished surface, so its surface tension pulls it into spheres.

Water dripping from a tap is pulled down by the force of gravity, but the water is also pulled into itself by surface tension, causing drops that look like stretched spheres.

The neuston

On flat surfaces of water, surface tension provides a barrier at the surface, which acts like a protective film if it is not broken. Animals that are heavier than water can walk on the surface tension provided that they do not get wet. A large number of animals, including spiders and insects, make their home on the surface tension. Collectively, these animals are known as the neuston. They must be very careful never to get themselves wet or they will sink and drown.

Water skaters live on the surface of rivers and ponds, hunting other small animals and walking on the surface tension.

Project Make a paperclip float on water

The paperclip floats on the surface and the water bulges around it. The water also bulges at the edges of the glass due to surface tension.

A paperclip is made of metal, which is denser than water, but you can make it float using surface tension. First rub the paperclip in your fingers to cover it with some oils from your skin. This will stop it getting wet. Fill a glass with water. Place the paperclip on a piece of tissue paper and carefully lay the tissue paper on the surface of the water. The tissue paper will soak with water and sink to the bottom, leaving the paperclip floating at the surface.

*Using different states

We use the qualities of different states of matter in many ways. Gases can be compressed, while liquids cannot. Solids can be mixed together by melting them.

Scuba divers breathe a special oxygen-rich mix of air that is stored under pressure in the aqualung.

▌Compressed gas

Gases can be compressed into small spaces by putting them under pressure. Scuba divers carry air to breathe underwater in a tank on their backs called an aqualung. The air in the aqualung is kept under pressure so that enough can fit in the tank for the diver to breathe for an hour or longer. Compressed gas is also used to power machines, a process known as pneumatics. Compressing air uses a lot of energy. In fact, 10 per cent of all the electricity used by industry in Europe is used to produce compressed air.

Making alloys

A bronze helmet made by the ancient Greeks about 500 BCE.

Mixing metals together can give them special qualities. These mixtures are called alloys. Alloys are made by heating the metals until they melt and mixing them together as liquids. Once they cool, they solidify into the new metal alloy. One of the first alloys humans made was bronze, which is a mix of copper and tin. Bronze is a very good metal for making tools and armour as it is hard and strong. Its use quickly caught on after it was discovered over 5,000 years ago, giving rise to a period known as the Bronze Age.

Hydraulics

Liquids cannot be compressed under pressure, but keep the same volume. This means that fluids can be used to transfer a force from one place to another. Machines that work using liquids are called hydraulic machines. A liquid in a tube is forced farther into the tube using a solid such as a piston at one end of the tube, which forces a piston at the other end of the tube out. The tube may be any shape and the force will be transferred, which means that you can change the direction of the force you are applying using hydraulics. Machines such as cranes, bulldozers and the brakes in cars work in this way.

The force from a crane's engine is transferred to the arm using hydraulics.

*Glossary

Altitude
Height above sea level.

Atom
The smallest particle of the basic elements. An atom is itself made of smaller subatomic particles called protons, neutrons and electrons.

Compress
To squeeze into a smaller volume. Gases can easily be compressed, but liquids and solids cannot.

Deflate
To let gas out of an object such as a balloon or a tyre.

Density
A measure of the compactness of a substance. The denser the substance, the more a given volume of it weighs.

Dissolve
The process by which a substance combines with a liquid to form a solution.

Electrical charge
A property of subatomic particles that produces electricity.

Energy
A measure of the amount of potential force that a substance contains.

Gravity
A force that pulls objects towards each other.

Horizontal
At the same angle as the horizon; flat.

Matter
The stuff from which all objects are made.

Molecule
A particle made of more than one atom, which is the smallest unit of a particular chemical.

Pigment
A substance used to make a particular colour, which is mixed with oil or water to make paint.

Pressure
A force caused, for instance, by the molecules of a gas confined in one area.

Suspension
An even mix of solid particles in a fluid. Over time, the particles will settle out from the fluid.

Water vapour
The gaseous form of water found in air.

*Resources

The Way Science Works, by Robin Kerrod and Dr Sharon Ann Holgate (DK, 2008)
Ideas for experiments, plus explanations of scientific theories. Produced in association with the Science Museum.

Essential Science: All About Gases, by Peter Riley (Franklin Watts, 2006)
The science behind gases, and how they can be both useful and harmful to us.

Essential Science: Solids and Liquids, by Peter Riley (Franklin Watts, 2006)
Experiment ideas and questions to see how much you know about solids and liquids.

Do Try This At Home! by Punk Science (Children's Books, 2008)
ISBN 9780230707412
Experiment ideas for 'punk scientists', with a DVD of the experiments.

Richard Hammond's Blast Lab, by Richard Hammond (DK, 2009)
The TV presenter shows how to do the experiments he carried out on his science show *Blast Lab*.

The Horrible Science of Everything, by Nick Arnold and Tony De Saulles (Scholastic, 2008)
An exploration of the yucky side of science.

Websites

www.bbc.co.uk/schools/ks2bitesize
Games, quizzes and revision notes on a wide range of science topics.

www.sciencemuseum.org.uk
The website of London's Science Museum, with features on the history of science and the latest scientific discoveries.

www.sciencewithme.com
Games and science project ideas, with worksheets and colouring books to print out.

www.scienceprojectideas.co.uk
Ideas for simple projects that you can do at home.

www.ratlab.co.uk
Project ideas with an explanation of the theory behind each one.

www.childrensuniversity.manchester.ac.uk
Scientists from the University of Manchester answer questions about all kinds of science topics.

*Index